TV **COOKS**

Ken Hom
COOKS
Chinese

Photographs by Philip Webb

Published by BBC Books,
an imprint of BBC Worldwide Publishing.
BBC Worldwide Limited, Woodlands,
80 Wood Lane, London W12 0TT.

The recipes in this book first appeared in the following:
Ken Hom's Illustrated Chinese Cookery
©Taurom Incorporated 1993
Ken Hom's Quick and Easy Chinese Cookery
©Taurom Incorporated 1989
Ken Hom's Vegetarian Cookery
©Taurom Incorporated 1987 and 1995

This edition first published 1996
© Taurom Incorporated 1996
The moral right of the author has been asserted

ISBN 0 563 38797 1

Edited by Pam Mallender
Designed by DW Design
Photographs by Philip Webb
Styling by Helen Payne
Home Economist Jane Stevenson

Set in New Caledonia and Helvetica
Printed and bound in Belgium by Proost NV
Colour separations by Colour Origination Ltd, London
Cover printed in Belgium by Proost NV

Cover and frontispiece: Sweet and Sour Prawns.

CONTENTS

RECIPE NOTES

Eggs are size 2.
Wash all fresh produce before preparation and peel as necessary.
Spoon measurements are level. Always use proper measuring spoons:
1 tb = 5ml and 1 tb = 15ml. Never mix metric or imperial measures in one recipe – stick to one or the other.

HANDY CONVERSION TABLES

Weight		Volume		Linear	
15g	½oz	30ml	1fl oz	5mm	¼in
25g	1oz	50ml	2fl oz	10mm/1cm	½in
40g	1½oz	100ml	3½fl oz	2cm	¾in
55g	2oz	125ml	4fl oz	2.5cm	1in
85g	3oz	150ml	5fl oz (¼ pint)	5cm	2in
115g	4oz	175ml	6fl oz	7.5cm	3in
140g	5oz	200ml	7fl oz (⅓ pint)	10cm	4in
175g	6oz	225ml	8fl oz	13cm	5in
200g	7oz	250ml	9fl oz	15cm	6in
225g	8oz	300ml	10fl oz (½ pint)	18cm	7in
250g	9oz	350ml	12fl oz	20cm	8in
280g	10oz	400ml	14fl oz	23cm	9in
350g	12oz	425ml	15fl oz (¾ pint)	25cm	10in
375g	13oz	450ml	16fl oz	28cm	11in
400g	14oz	500ml	18fl oz	30cm	12in
425g	15oz	600ml	20fl oz (1 pint)		
450g	1lb	700ml	1¼ pints	**Oven temperatures**	
550g	1¼lb	850ml	1½ pints	225F	110C	GAS ¼
750g	1lb 10oz	1 litre	1¾ pints	250F	120C	GAS ½
900g	2lb	1.2 litres	2 pints	275F	140C	GAS 1
1kg	2¼lb	1.3 litres	2¼ pints	300F	150C	GAS 2
1.3kg	3lb	1.4 litres	2½ pints	325F	160C	GAS 3
1.8kg	4lb	1.7 litres	3 pints	350F	180C	GAS 4
2.25kg	5lb	2 litres	3½ pints	375F	190C	GAS 5
		2.5 litres	4½ pints	400F	200C	GAS 6
				425F	220C	GAS 7
				450F	230C	GAS 8
				475F	240C	GAS 9

SERVING NOTES

Traditionally, Chinese meals always consist of a soup, a rice, noodle or bread dish, a vegetable dish and at least two other dishes which may be mainly meat, fish or chicken. Soup is not drunk as a first course as in the West but throughout the meal. The dishes are all served together and placed in the centre of the table.

The recipes in this book are based on the expectation that you will cook two main dishes per meal. If you prefer to cook just one such dish then you will need to double the quantities given in the recipe.

Ⓥ   **Suitable for vegetarians**   ✷   **Suitable for freezing**

Ⓛ   **Low fat**

Welcome to the exciting world of Chinese cookery! It is a world full of aromatic aromas and flavours and is fun to prepare.

The recipes in this book are a selection of some of the easiest and quickest dishes that I make daily in my personal life. Years ago, when I had more time and inclination, I made more elaborate meals with many courses. I am still very interested in good food but find myself increasingly occupied with my work and career. So I have evolved a quick and easy method of cooking, drawing from my Chinese background, but with no compromise as far as quality is concerned.

Good fresh ingredients continue to be a primary concern of mine. I have only taken short cuts in preparation techniques and substituted some ingredients, but have always used authentic seasonings and spices to get the right taste. You will also find special tips with each recipe to guide you along the way.

I don't believe that fast cooking means bad cooking. It is a matter of organisation, choice of recipe and experience. It is much easier than you think.

These recipes have been specially edited for convenience and ease of use so that you can serve good food in no time at all. There are recipes for all seasons and with the wide availability of speciality ingredients in supermarkets these days, there is really no excuse for not making simply delicious meals.

I wish you Happy Cooking and Good Health!

INGREDIENTS

Chillies

Fresh chillies: these should look fresh and bright with no brown patches or black spots. Red chillies are generally milder than green because they sweeten as they ripen.

Dried chillies: small, thin and about 1cm/½in long, these are commonly used to season oil for stir-fried dishes, added to sauces and when braising.

Coriander (Chinese parsley)

One of the relatively few herbs used in Chinese cookery, coriander has a pungent, musky, citrus-like flavour. Look for deep green, fresh-looking leaves.

Sauces and pastes

Hoisin sauce: sweet and spicy, this is a thick, dark, brownish-red sauce made from soya beans, vinegar, sugar, spices and other flavourings.

Soy sauces: these are an essential ingredient in Chinese cooking. They are made from a mixture of soya beans, flour and water which is fermented naturally and aged for some months. The distilled liquid is soy sauce. Light soy sauce is better for cooking. Dark soy sauce is more mature, thicker and stronger and more suitable for stews or as a dipping sauce.

Whole yellow bean sauce: made from yellow beans fermented with flour and salt, it is quite salty. There are two forms: whole beans in a thick sauce and mashed or puréed beans (sold as Crushed yellow bean sauce). The whole bean variety is slighlty less salty and has a better texture.

Sesame oil

Thick, rich, golden-brown, this is made from sesame seeds and has a nutty flavour and aroma. It is widely used as a seasoning, and added at the last moment to finish a dish because it heats rapidly and burns easily.

Shaoxing rice wine

Made from glutinous rice, yeast and spring water, this is used extensively for cooking and drinking throughout China. Do not confuse it with sake, the Japanese version of rice wine. It is available in Chinese supermarkets and some wine shops. It should be kept tightly corked at room temperature. A good quality, dry sherry can be substituted.

Vinegars

Vinegars are widely used in Chinese cooking. Unlike Western vinegars, Chinese vinegars are usually made from rice. They range in flavour from spicy and slightly tart, to sweet and pungent.

White rice vinegar: clear and mild in flavour it is used for sweet and sour dishes.

Black rice vinegar: dark and rich, it is mild in taste and used for braised dishes, sauces and sometimes as a dipping sauce for crab.

Water chestnuts

Fresh water chestnuts are a white and crunchy sweet root vegetable or bulb about the size of a walnut. They will keep, unpeeled, in a paper bag in the fridge for up to two weeks. Peel before use and if you have any left-over, place them back in the fridge covered with cold water. Canned water chestnuts have a good texture but little taste. Rinse well before using. Store any unused ones in a jar of cold water. They will keep for several weeks in the fridge if you change the water daily.

EQUIPMENT

Chopping boards
Use a hardwood or white acrylic chopping board and clean after use with vinegar or lemon. The Chinese traditionally use a soft wood block but they are difficult to maintain and keep clean.

Chopsticks
These are not just used for eating, they are also used as a combination spoon and fork for stirring, beating, whipping and mixing. Special long chopsticks are available for these tasks.

Cleaver
Most chefs rely on three different sizes – light, medium and heavy. If you decide to invest in a cleaver, choose a good stainless steel model and keep it sharpened. Once you've become proficient you will see how it can be used on all types of food to slice, dice, chop, fillet, shred and crush.

Rice cookers
These cook rice perfectly and keep it warm throughout the meal. They are relatively expensive, so unless you eat rice frequently I do not think they are worth the expense.

Steamers
Bamboo steamers come in several sizes of which the 25cm/10in is the most suitable for home use. The food is placed in the steamer which is placed above boiling water in a wok or pot. Several can be stacked for multiple cooking. Before using for the first time, wash it, then steam empty for about 5 minutes. Any kind of wide, metal steamer can be used, if you prefer.

Wok
Choosing: select a wok preferably 30-35cm/12-14in in diameter with deep sides. It should feel heavy and if possible, be made of carbon steel. Light stainless steel and aluminium tend to scorch.
Seasoning: all woks (except non-stick) need to be seasoned. Many also need to be scrubbed first to remove the oil used to protect them in transit. This is the only time you will scrub your wok – unless you let it rust up. Use a cream cleanser and water to remove as much oil as possible, dry it, then place on the hob over a low heat. Add two tablespoons of cooking oil (do not use olive oil) and, using kitchen paper, rub it over the inside of the wok until lightly coated with oil. Heat slowly for about 20 minutes, then wipe thoroughly with kitchen paper. Repeat processes until the paper wipes clean. Cleaning: once seasoned, wash in clean water and dry by putting over a low heat for a few minutes.

Wok accessories
Wok stand: this can be a metal ring with ventilation holes or a circular thin wire frame designed to keep a conventionally-shaped wok steady on the hob. It is essential if you want to use your wok for steaming, deep-frying or braising. If you have a gas cooker, use only the latter type.
Wok lid: this light, domed cover is usually made from aluminium and used when steaming.
Spatula: shaped like a small shovel this is long-handled and ideal for scooping and tossing food.
Rack: when steaming you will need a wooden or metal rack or trivet to raise the food to be cooked above the water level. Wok sets normally include one. If yours does not, you could use a small empty can to support the plate of food.
Bamboo brush: this bundle of stiff, split bamboo is used for cleaning a wok without scrubbing off the seasoned surface. It is not essential, a soft washing-up brush will do.

1 Black rice vinegar

2 White rice vinegar

3 Shaoxing rice wine

4 Coriander

5 Whole yellow bean sauce

6 Bok choy

7 Fresh root ginger

8 Chinese dried mushrooms

9 Fresh water chestnuts

10 Dried black mushrooms

11 Dried cloudear mushrooms

12 Thin egg noodles

13 Rounded egg noodles

14 Salted black beans

15 Hoisin sauce

16 Papaya

17 Canned straw mushrooms

18 Sesame paste

19 Beancurd

20 Chinese leaves

21 Bean thread noodles

22 Thin rice noodles

23 Mango

1. Electric rice cooker
2. Wide metal steamer
3. Wok lid
4. Rack
5. Wok stand
6. Carbon steel wok
7. Stainless steel cleaver
8. Acrylic chopping board
9. Bamboo steamer
10. Chopsticks (for eating)
11. Long chopsticks (for cooking)
12. Spatula
13. Bamboo brush

Starters & Appetisers

GRILLED PRAWNS WITH FRESH CORIANDER AND GINGER SAUCE

These prawns also cook wonderfully on a barbecue and can be served as an elegant cold buffet dish or as a quick and easy lunch.

Serves 2–4

450g/1lb fresh raw prawns, peeled and deveined (See Tip)

FOR THE MARINADE

1 tbsp light soy sauce

1 tsp Shaoxing rice wine or dry sherry

1 tsp sesame oil

FOR THE SAUCE

2 tbsp finely chopped fresh coriander

2 tsp white rice vinegar

1 tsp finely chopped fresh root ginger

1 Preheat the grill and pat the prawns dry on kitchen paper. Combine the marinade ingredients, add the prawns and set aside for 10 minutes. Mix together the sauce ingredients. Lay the prawns on a baking tray, grill for 3 minutes on one side, then for 2 minutes on the other side. Serve with the sauce.

Nutrition notes per serving for two: *115 calories, Protein 20g, Carbohydrate 1g, Fat 3g, Saturated fat 1g, Fibre none, Added sugar none, Salt 3.50g.*

TIP

To peel prawns: first twist off the head and pull off the tail, then peel off the body shell and tiny legs. To devein: using a small sharp knife, partially split the prawns lengthways and remove the fine digestive cord.

CHINESE BARBECUED CHICKEN WINGS ✻

Prepare ahead, leave covered in the fridge and return to room temperature before cooking.

Serves 4

900g chicken wings

FOR THE BARBECUE SAUCE

2 tbsp dark soy sauce

3 tbsp hoisin sauce

2 large garlic cloves

1 tbsp chopped fresh root ginger

1 tbsp Shaoxing rice wine or dry sherry

1 tbsp sesame oil

2 tsp chilli bean sauce

2 tsp sugar

1 Preheat the oven to 475F/240C/Gas 9. Place the chicken wings in an ovenproof dish. Combine the barbecue sauce ingredients in a blender and process for 5 seconds. Pour over the chicken and toss to coat thoroughly. Cook for 15 minutes, then reduce the heat to 350F/180C/Gas 4 and cook for a further 20 minutes. Serve hot or cool and serve at room temperature.

Nutrition notes per serving: *324 calories, Protein 23g, Carbohydrate 7g, Fat 22g, Saturated fat 6g, Fibre 1g, Added sugar 3g, Salt 0.51g.*

✻ *Cool quickly, then freeze. Can be frozen for up to 1 month. To serve, defrost in the fridge, then reheat until piping hot.*

Soups

SWEETCORN SOUP WITH CRABMEAT

This reheats well. Use canned or frozen sweetcorn, thawed, if you prefer.

Serves 4

1 egg white

1 tsp sesame oil

1.2 litres/2 pints Chicken stock
(page 62)

280g/10oz fresh sweetcorn kernels

1 tbsp Shaoxing rice wine (page 7)

1 tbsp light soy sauce

2 tsp finely chopped fresh root ginger

1 tsp salt

¼ tsp freshly ground white pepper

1 tsp sugar

2 tsp cornflour

225g/8oz crabmeat

chopped spring onions, to garnish

1 Mix the egg white and sesame oil in a bowl and set aside. Bring the stock to the boil in a large pan, add the corn and simmer, uncovered, for 15 minutes.

2 Add the rice wine, soy sauce, ginger, salt, pepper, sugar and cornflour blended with two teaspoons of water to the pan. Bring back to the boil, then lower the heat to a simmer. Add the crabmeat, then slowly pour in the egg white mixture in a steady stream, stirring all the time. Serve garnished with the spring onions.

Nutrition notes per serving: *197 calories, Protein 16g, Carbohydrate 23g, Fat 5g, Saturated fat 1g, Fibre 1g, Added sugar 6g, Salt 3.26g.*

TIP

To remove fresh sweetcorn kernels from the cob: pull off the stem, surrounding leaves and silky fibres. Hold the cob upright on a work surface and working downwards, cut off the corn with a sharp knife or cleaver.

TOMATO EGGFLOWER SOUP

This impressive looking soup is especially delightful in summer made with fresh tomatoes.

Serves 4

1.2 litres/2 pints Chicken stock
(page 62)

1 tsp sugar

1 tsp salt

1 tbsp light soy sauce

225g/8oz fresh tomatoes, skinned, seeded and cut into 2.5cm/1in cubes

3 tbsp chopped spring onions, white parts only, use green parts to garnish

2 eggs

2 tsp sesame oil

1 Place the stock in a pan and bring to a simmer. Add the sugar, salt and soy sauce and mix well. Add the tomatoes and simmer for 2 minutes, then stir in the white spring onion parts.

2 Lightly beat the eggs with the sesame oil. Add to the pan in a very slow, thin stream. Using a chopstick or fork, pull the egg slowly into strands. (I have found that stirring the egg in a figure of eight works quite well.) Garnish and serve.

Nutrition notes per serving: *78 calories, Protein 5g, Carbohydrate 4g, Fat 5g, Saturated fat 1g, Fibre 1g, Added sugar 1g, Salt 2.36g.*

Ⓥ Vegetarian option: *replace the chicken stock with vegetable stock.*

CHICKEN WITH RICE NOODLES IN SOUP

Perfect for a cold winter's day. Add other vegetables for a more substantial meal. If you like spicy soup, stir in a teaspoon or two of chilli bean sauce and perhaps one and a half teaspoons of fresh lemon or lime juice.

Serves 4–6

1.2 litres/2 pints Chicken stock (page 62)

115g boneless chicken breast, finely shredded

115g/4oz dried rice noodles

1 tsp salt

2 tsp sesame oil

2 spring onions, finely chopped, to garnish

1 Bring the stock to a simmer. Add the chicken and rice noodles and simmer for 5 minutes or until the chicken is just cooked through. Add the salt and sesame oil and serve garnished with the spring onions.

Nutrition notes per serving: *168 calories, Protein 11g, Carbohydrate 22g, Fat 5g, Saturated fat 1g, Fibre 1g, Added sugar none, Salt 2.27g.*

TRI-COLOUR SOUP

Colourful and appetising, this soup makes a great starter and can double as a main dish for a quick family meal. Other vegetables such as Chinese flowering cabbage, Chinese leaves or Swiss chard, can be used instead of spinach.

Serves 4–6

1.2 litres/2 pints Chicken stock (page 62)

225g/8oz fresh tomatoes, halved horizontally, seeded and coarsely chopped, or canned tomatoes, drained and roughly chopped

225g/8oz firm beancurd, cut into 1cm/½in pieces (See Tip)

225g/8oz fresh spinach, stalks removed

1 tbsp light soy sauce

½ tsp freshly ground white or black pepper

½ tsp sugar

½ tsp white rice vinegar

1 Bring the stock to a simmer. Add the tomatoes, beancurd and spinach leaves and simmer for 2 minutes. Add the remaining ingredients, give the soup several gentle stirs and serve.

Nutrition notes per serving: *78 calories, Protein 8g, Carbohydrate 5g, Fat 3g, Saturated fat 1g, Fibre 2g, Added sugar 1g, Salt 1.20g.*

Ⓥ **Vegetarian option:** *replace the chicken stock with vegetable stock*

TIP

Beancurd has a distinctive texture but a bland taste. It is made from yellow soya beans which are soaked, ground, mixed with water, then cooked briefly before being solidified. It is usually sold as firm cakes for stir-frying, braising and poaching or as a thickish junket (sometimes called silken tofu, for soups). It is also available dried and fermented. To use solid white beancurd 'cakes', carefully cut the amount required into cubes or shreds using a sharp knife. It is delicate and care should also be taken when cooking, too much stirring can cause it to crumble. Whatever its shape or texture, it remains highly nutritious.

Meat

FIVE-SPICE SPARERIBS ✸

These spareribs are marinated, deep-fried, then slowly braised in a piquant sauce. The taste improves if they are cooked the day before eaten. Five-spice powder is a mixture of star anise, Sichuan peppercorns, fennel, cloves and cinnamon.

Serves 4

750g pork spareribs, separated and cut into 7.5cm/3in chunks

600ml/1 pint groundnut (peanut) oil for deep-frying (See Tip page 20)

FOR THE MARINADE

1 tbsp Shaoxing rice wine or dry sherry

1 tbsp light soy sauce

1 tbsp Chinese black rice vinegar or cider vinegar

2 tsp sesame oil

1 tbsp cornflour

FOR THE SAUCE

2 tbsp finely chopped garlic

2 tsp five-spice powder

3 tbsp finely chopped spring onions

3 tbsp Chinese rock sugar, white sugar or chunky amber coffee sugar crystals

3 tbsp Shaoxing rice wine or dry sherry

150ml/¼ pint Chicken stock (page 62)

1½ tbsp light soy sauce

2 tbsp dried grated orange peel (See Tip)

85ml/3fl oz Chinese black rice vinegar or cider vinegar

1   Mix together the marinade ingredients and marinate the spareribs for 25 minutes at room temperature. Remove using a slotted spoon.

2   Heat the oil in a deep-fat fryer or large wok until slightly smoking and slowly brown the spareribs, in batches, then drain on kitchen paper. (Leave the oil to cool and strain through a filter if you want to re-use when cooking pork.)

3   Place the sauce ingredients in a clean wok or frying pan, bring to the boil, then reduce the heat. Add the spareribs, cover and gently simmer for 40 minutes, stirring occasionally. If necessary, add a little water to the sauce to prevent the spareribs from drying up. Skim off any surface fat and serve.

Nutrition notes per serving: *737 calories, Protein 24g, Carbohydrate 19g, Fat 61g, Saturated fat 22g, Fibre 1g, Added sugar 12g, Salt 0.42g.*

✸ *Cool quickly, then freeze. Can be frozen for up to 1 month. To serve, defrost in the fridge, then reheat until piping hot.*

TIP

To make dried orange peel: peel the skin off an orange, scraping away as much of the white pith as possible or coarsely grate the peel. Lay on kitchen paper and dry in the sun, an airing cupboard or in a warm, but turned off oven, until dry and very hard. Store in a tightly-sealed container in a cool dry place. To use, soak the required amount in warm water until it softens, then chop or slice according to the recipe. Add grated peel to dishes without soaking first.

SWEET AND SOUR PORK

Of all Chinese dishes, this is probably one of the best known in the West and unfortunately rarely properly made. Properly prepared, sweet and sour dishes are so delicately balanced it is difficult to describe them as either strictly sweet or sour. In my version you will find that balance. This is best served with plain Steamed rice (page 62) and a simple blanched vegetable such as cabbage or Chinese leaves in soy sauce (page 44).

Serves 4

450g lean pork, cut into 2.5cm/1in cubes

1 tbsp Shaoxing rice wine or dry sherry

1 tbsp light soy sauce

2 tsp sesame oil

½ tsp salt

1 egg, beaten

2 tbsp cornflour

450ml/16fl oz groundnut (peanut) oil for deep-frying (See Tip)

85g/3oz canned lychees, drained or fresh orange segments

FOR THE SAUCE

115g/4oz carrots, cut into 2.5cm/1in pieces

150ml/¼ pint Chicken stock (page 62)

1 tbsp light soy sauce

2 tsp dark soy sauce

2 tsp sesame oil

½ tsp salt

1 tsp freshly ground white pepper

1½ tbsp Chinese white rice vinegar or cider vinegar

1 tbsp sugar

2 tbsp tomato purée or ketchup

1 green and 1 red pepper (each about 115g/4oz), cut into 2.5cm/1in squares

55g/2oz spring onions, cut into 2.5cm/1in pieces

2 tsp cornflour blended with 1 tbsp water

1 Place the pork in a bowl with the rice wine, light soy sauce, sesame oil and salt and marinate for 20 minutes. Meanwhile, blanch the carrots for the sauce in boiling water for 4 minutes, then drain.

2 In a bowl, mix together the egg and cornflour until blended to a batter. Lift the pork cubes out of the marinade, dust with cornflour, then place in the batter and coat each piece well.

3 Heat the oil in a deep-fat fryer or large wok until slightly smoking. Using a slotted spoon, remove the pork pieces from the batter and deep-fry until golden. Drain on kitchen paper.

4 Make the sauce: combine the stock, soy sauces, sesame oil, salt, pepper, vinegar, sugar and tomato purée in a large pan and bring to the boil. Add the carrots, peppers and spring onions and stir well. Stir in the cornflour mixture and bring back to the boil. Reduce heat to a simmer, then add the lychees and pork cubes. Mix well and serve.

Nutrition notes per serving: *382 calories, Protein 28g, Carbohydrate 27g, Fat 18g, Saturated fat 5g, Fibre 2g, Added sugar 4g, Salt 1.71g.*

TIP

Groundnut (peanut) oil: this has a pleasant, unobtrusive taste and can be heated to a high temperature making it perfect for stir-frying and deep-frying. If you cannot find it, use corn oil instead. When deep-frying, you may find deep-fat fryers safer and easier to use than a wok. The quantities of oil in recipes is based on the amount required for deep-frying in a wok. If using a deep-fat fryer, you will need about double the amount, but never fill it more than half-full with oil.

BEEF IN OYSTER SAUCE

One of the most popular dishes in our family restaurant, this is delicious served with plain Steamed rice (page 62) and Chinese leaves in soy sauce (page 44). It also goes well with Sweetcorn soup with crabmeat (page 15). A good brand of oyster sauce, made from a concentrate of oysters cooked in soy sauce and brine, does not taste fishy. Rather, it has a meaty taste and goes very well with beef or pork. It has a rich flavour and is also used as a condiment, diluted with a little oil, for vegetables, poultry and meats.

Serves 4

450g lean beef steak, cut into 5cm/2in long thin slices (See Tip)

1 tbsp light soy sauce

2 tsp sesame oil

1 tbsp Shaoxing rice wine or dry sherry

2 tsp cornflour

3 tbsp groundnut (peanut) oil

3 tbsp oyster sauce

1½ tbsp finely shredded spring onions, to garnish

1 Place the beef in a bowl, add the soy sauce, sesame oil, rice wine and cornflour, then leave to marinate for 20 minutes.

2 Heat a wok or large frying pan until very hot, pour in the oil and when it is slightly smoking, add the beef slices and stir fry for 5 minutes or until they are lightly browned all over. Remove and drain well in a colander set inside a bowl. Discard the oil.

3 Wipe the wok or frying pan clean and reheat over a high heat until it is hot. Add the oyster sauce and bring to a simmer. Return the beef slices to the pan and toss thoroughly with the sauce. Transfer to a plate, garnish and serve.

Nutrition notes per serving: *229 calories, Protein 24g, Carbohydrate 5g, Fat 12g, Saturated fat 3g, Fibre trace, Added sugar trace, Salt 1.37g.*

TIP

I prefer fillet steak for stir frying since it is lean and tender and full of flavour. Although it is expensive, a little goes a long way. Sirloin, rump and T-bone steak are also suitable. To slice the beef, hold firmly on the chopping board with one hand and slice the straight down into very thin slices. Meat is always sliced across the grain to break up the fibres and to make it more tender when it is cooked. If you use a cleaver rather than a knife for this, hold the cleaver with your index finger over the far side of the top of the cleaver and your thumb on the side nearest you to guide the cutting edge firmly. Hold the food with your other hand, turning your fingers under for safety. Your knuckles should act as a guide for the blade of the knife or cleaver.

HOT AND TANGY MINCED LAMB

This dish, in which the flavours of East and West meet, readily combines with pasta, rice, noodles or even bread to make a quick, easy and substantial meal in less than 30 minutes. You can use minced beef, if you prefer. Sesame paste is a rich, thick, creamy brown paste made from roasted sesame seeds and should not be confused with the Middle Eastern tahini. If you cannot find it, use a smooth peanut butter.

Serves 4–6

1 tbsp groundnut (peanut) oil

450g minced lamb (See Tip)

3 tbsp coarsely chopped garlic

2 tbsp coarsely chopped fresh root ginger

2 tbsp tomato purée

2 tbsp sesame paste

1½ tbsp dark soy sauce

1 tbsp fresh lemon juice

1 tbsp chilli bean sauce

2 tsp sugar

1 tbsp Shaoxing rice wine or dry sherry

1 Heat a wok or large frying pan, then add the oil and lamb. Stir fry for 2 minutes and add the garlic and ginger. Continue cooking for 1 minute, then stir in the tomato purée, sesame paste, soy sauce, lemon juice, chilli bean sauce, sugar and rice wine. (You will find it quicker, when required to add a number of ingredients at the same time as in this recipe, to measure them all into one bowl and add them in one go.) Cook for 4 minutes, then serve.

Nutrition notes per serving for four: *292 calories, Protein 27g, Carbohydrate 7g, Fat 17g, Saturated fat 6g, Fibre 1g, Added sugar 3g, Salt 0.31g.*

TIP

I prefer to use meat which has not been frozen since freezing breaks down the cell structure and makes it watery when it is thawed; besides I think fresh meat has a better flavour. This is particularly important when selecting meat for stir-frying. The meat should be as dry as possible so that it will fry rather than steam in its own juices. You can buy your lamb or beef, if using, already minced. Or you may like to mince your own. Use loin chops with the bones and all the fat removed, lamb fillets (which come from the neck) and lamb steaks. Mincing is a fine-chopping technique. Chefs use two cleavers to mince, rapidly chopping them in unison for fast results. One cleaver or knife is easier for the less expert, although the process will, of course, take a little longer. First slice the meat, then using a sharp knife or cleaver, rapidly chop the food until it is rather spread out over the chopping board. Scrape it into a pile, chop again and continue chopping until the meat reaches the required texture. You may find it easier to hold the knife or cleaver by the top of the blade (rather than by the handle) with two hands, as though you were chopping parsley. A food processor can also be used but be careful not to over-mince or you will lose texture and taste.

Poultry

GARLIC CHICKEN WITH CUCUMBER

Cucumbers are rarely served raw in China; they are delicious cooked. This is an uncomplicated dish which goes well with the Tomato eggflower soup (page 15). Chilli bean sauce is a thick, dark sauce or paste made from soya beans, chillies and other seasonings. It varies from mildy hot to very hot and spicy depending on the brand. In this recipe they are stir fried with delicate chicken breasts and flavoured with garlic and chilli.

Serves 4

450g/1lb cucumber

2 tsp salt

1 tbsp groundnut (peanut) oil

450g boneless skinless chicken breasts, cut into 2.5cm/1cm cubes

1½ tbsp finely chopped garlic

1 tbsp finely chopped spring onions

1 tbsp light soy sauce

1 tbsp Shaoxing rice wine or dry sherry

2 tsp chilli bean sauce or chilli powder

2 tsp sesame oil

1   Peel the cucumber, halve and remove the seeds with a teaspoon. Cut into 2.5cm/1in cubes, sprinkle with salt and place in a colander to drain for 20 minutes. (Cucumbers are 96 per cent water. Salting them removes excess moisture.) Rinse the cubes under cold running water, then carefully blot dry with kitchen paper.

2   Heat a wok or large frying pan, then add the oil and when slightly smoking, add the chicken cubes and stir fry for a few seconds. Add all the remaining ingredients, except the cucumber, and stir fry for a further 2 minutes. Add the cucumber, stir fry for 3 minutes, then serve.

Nutrition notes per serving: *193 calories, Protein 26g, Carbohydrate 3g, Fat 8g, Saturated fat 2g, Fibre 1g, Added sugar trace, Salt 0.71g.*

TIP

Stir frying is the most famous of all Chinese cooking techniques and it is possibly the trickiest, since success depends upon having all the required ingredients prepared, measured out and immediately at hand and on having a good source of fierce heat. Its advantage is that, properly executed, stir fried foods can be cooked in minutes in very little oil so they retain their natural flavours and textures. It is very important that stir fried foods are not overcooked or made greasy – and it is surprising how easy it is to do this. But keep trying because once you have mastered this technique you will find that it becomes your favourite technique. Using a wok is definitely an advantage when stir frying as its shape not only conducts the heat well but its high sides enable you to toss the stir fry ingredients rapidly, keeping them constantly moving while cooking.

CHICKEN THIGH CASSEROLE WITH ORANGE ⊛

The Chinese prefer to buy their chickens live to ensure that they are at their freshest when cooked. Obviously, this is not practical in the West. Commercially-produced chickens tend to lack taste and frozen chicken is especially bland and should be avoided whenever possible. Try to buy a fresh chicken for Chinese cooking. It should have a healthy pinkish colour, a fresh smell and be firm in texture. If possible buy free-range or corn-fed – not only have they been raised by more humane methods but their taste is far superior. All parts of the chicken are used in China. The dark meat from the thighs and drumsticks is especially prized for its sturdier flavour. This is an 'overnighter'. My mother used to make this dish the night before and simply reheat it the next day. She used dried orange peel but I like the clean taste of fresh oranges. The easiest way to remove rind thinly is with a vegetable peeler. Pile the resulting pieces on top of each other and cut into thin strips with a sharp knife.

Serves 4

1½ tbsp groundnut (peanut) oil

900g skinless chicken thighs

1 tbsp finely chopped garlic

1 tbsp finely chopped fresh root ginger

2 tbsp black beans, drained (See Tip)

2 tsp orange rind, cut into thin strips

150ml/¼ pint fresh orange juice

2 tbsp light soy sauce

2 tsp chilli bean sauce

1   Heat a large, heavy, flameproof casserole, then add the oil and quickly brown the chicken thighs on both sides. Push to the side of the casserole, then add the garlic, ginger, black beans and orange rind and stir for 30 seconds.

2   Add the orange juice, soy sauce and chilli bean sauce, bring to the boil, then lower the heat to a simmer. Cover the casserole tightly and cook for 20 minutes or until the chicken is done. Check by piercing with a skewer, the juices should run clear.

Nutrition notes per serving: *210 calories, Protein 23g, Carbohydrate 6g, Fat 11g, Saturated fat 3g, Fibre 1g, Added sugar none, Salt 0.26g.*

⊛ *Cool quickly, then freeze. Can be frozen for up to 1 month. To serve, defrost in the fridge, then reheat thoroughly until piping hot.*

TIP

Small black soya beans, also known as salted black beans, are preserved by being fermented with salt and spices. They have a slightly salty taste and a pleasant, rich smell. They can be bought in tins or packed in plastic bags and are usually used whole or chopped.

SPICY CHICKEN WITH PEANUTS

Chicken is the most highly regarded of all poultry in China. To impress a guest a Chinese hostess might announce that she has killed a chicken in his or her honour. It is frequently served on special occasions, on birthdays and at festivals and banquets. At our family gatherings, chicken was always the centrepiece. In China most homes do not have ovens and poultry is usually roasted by professional cooks and sold in speciality food shops. Home-cooked chicken is braised, stir fried, deep-fried, steamed or simmered. One of the virtues of chicken is that its mild but distinctive flavour blends very well with other seasonings, spices and sauces. It is a very versatile bird and is as popular in China as pork. This dish is better known in China as Gongbao chicken. According to one legend, it was named after a Chinese official, Ding Baozhen, governor of Sichuan province in the 19th century. There are many versions of this recipe; this one is close to the original, in addition to being quick and easy to make.

Serves 4

1½ tbsp groundnut (peanut) oil

1 dried red chilli, split lengthways

225g boneless chicken breasts, cut into 2.5cm/1in cubes

85g/3oz raw peanuts, shelled and skinned (See Tip)

FOR THE SAUCE

1 tbsp Chicken stock (page 62)

1 tbsp Shaoxing rice wine or dry sherry

2 tsp dark soy sauce

1 tsp sugar

1 tsp finely chopped garlic

2 tsp finely sliced spring onions

½ tsp finely chopped fresh root ginger

1 tsp Chinese white rice vinegar 200or cider vinegar

½ tsp salt

1 tsp sesame oil

1 Heat a wok or large frying pan until very hot, add the oil and when slightly smoking, add the chilli and stir fry for a few seconds. (You can remove it when it turns black, or leave it in.) Add the chicken cubes and peanuts and stir fry for 1 minute, then remove everything from the pan.

2 Place all the sauce ingredients, except the sesame oil, in the pan, bring to the boil, then reduce the heat. Return the chicken, peanuts and chilli to the pan and cook, stirring, for 2 minutes or until the chicken is cooked. Add the sesame oil and give the mixture a good stir. Remove the chilli, transfer to a plate and serve.

Nutrition notes per serving: *244 calories, Protein 18g, Carbohydrate 5g, Fat 17g, Saturated fat 3g, Fibre 1g, Added sugar 1g, Salt 0.74g.*

TIP

To skin peanuts: immerse the shelled peanuts in a pan of boiling water for 2 minutes. Drain, let them cool and the thin red skins will rub off easily.

MANGO CHICKEN

This might be called 'Nouvelle Hong Kong' or South East Asia meets Hong Kong. It is an exotic and unlikely combination. I have eaten this dish several times in Hong Kong and found it delicious every time. The rich sweetness and soft texture of the mango works extremely well with the delicate taste of the chicken. The mango is cooked for a short time, just enough to warm it through. Mangoes are very popular in Hong Kong. They are imported from Thailand and the Philippines and are one of the best liked of all tropical fruits and, as this recipe indicates, mix well with other distinctively-flavoured foods.

Serves 4

450g boneless skinless chicken breasts, cut into 2.5cm/1in pieces

1 egg white

2 tsp sesame oil

2 tsp salt

2 tsp cornflour

freshly ground black pepper, to taste

600ml/1 pint groundnut (peanut) oil or water, plus 1½ tbsp groundnut (peanut) oil

1 tbsp finely chopped fresh root ginger

1 tbsp finely chopped garlic

1½ tbsp Shaoxing rice wine or dry sherry

2 mangoes, peeled and cut into 2.5cm/1in pieces (See Tip)

1 tbsp finely chopped fresh coriander, to garnish

1   Mix together the chicken, egg white, half the sesame oil, half the salt, the cornflour and pepper and chill for 20 minutes.

2   Heat a large wok or frying pan until very hot and pour in the groundnut oil. Heat until the oil is slightly smoking, then remove from the heat and add the chicken pieces, stirring vigorously to prevent them sticking. Cook for 2 minutes or until the chicken turns white, then drain the chicken and the oil in a stainless steel colander, set inside a bowl. Discard the oil. If using water, bring to the boil, then remove the pan from the heat and add the chicken, stirring vigorously. Cook for 2 minutes or until the chicken turns white, then drain.

3   Heat the remaining groundnut oil in the wok or pan, add the ginger and garlic and stir fry for 30 seconds. Add the rice wine, remaining sesame oil and salt and the mangoes. Stir fry gently for 2 minutes or until the mangoes are heated through. Add the chicken, heat through and mix well, garnish and serve.

Nutrition notes per serving: *319 calories, Protein 27g, Carbohydrate 28g, Fat 11g, Saturated fat 2g, Fibre 5g, Added sugar trace, Salt 2.73g.*

Ⓥ **Vegetarian option:** *substitute cubes of firm beancurd for the chicken, stir fry briefly in the oil until golden, drain, then add at the end of Step 3.*

TIP

To prepare mangoes: cut a large slice from one side of the fruit, close to the stone, then repeat on the other side. Cut the flesh in the slices lengthways and crossways without breaking the skin, push the skin inside out to expose the cubes of flesh and cut off cubes. Peel the remaining centre section, then using a sharp knife, cut the flesh away from the stone .

Fish & Shellfish

STEAMED FISH WITH GARLIC, SPRING ONIONS AND GINGER

Throughout the world, the consumption of all kinds of seafood has been rapidly growing over the past decade. Fish and shellfish are very nutritious and generally low in fat and cholesterol. In this preference for the 'harvest of the sea', the world is catching up to the well-established Chinese custom. Steaming is a great southern Chinese tradition and it is my favourite method of cooking fish as it preserves the purest flavours of the fish. As it is such a gentle cooking technique, nothing masks the fresh taste of the fish, which remains moist and tender and you can savour the combination of the other ingredients.

Serves 4

450g/1lb fresh, firm white fish fillets, such as cod, sea bass or sole or a whole fish such as sole or turbot, cleaned and gills removed (See Tip)

1 tsp coarse sea salt or plain salt

1½ tbsp finely shredded fresh root ginger

FOR THE GARNISH

3 tbsp finely shredded spring onions

1 tbsp light soy sauce

2 tsp dark soy sauce

1 tbsp groundnut (peanut) oil

2 tsp sesame oil

2 garlic cloves, thinly sliced

1 Pat the fish fillets or fish dry with kitchen paper. Rub with the salt on both sides, and set aside for 30 minutes. (This helps the flesh to firm up and draws out any excess moisture.)

2 Set up a steamer, or put a rack into a wok or deep pan and fill with 5cm/2in of water. Bring the water to the boil over a high heat, then reduce the heat. Put the fish on a heatproof plate and scatter the ginger evenly over the top.

3 Place the plate in the steamer or on to the rack. (The food needs to remain above the water level and must not get wet. The water level should always be at least 2.5cm/1in below the edge of the food plate.) Cover the pan tightly and gently steam the fish until just cooked. Flat fish will take about 5 minutes, thicker fish or fillets 12–14 minutes.

4 Remove the plate and fish and sprinkle over the spring onions and soy sauces. Heat the two oils in a small pan and when they are hot, add the garlic slices and brown them. Pour the garlic oil over the top of the fish and serve.

Nutrition notes per serving: 140 calories, Protein 21g, Carbohydrate 3g, Fat 5g, Saturated fat 1g, Fibre 1g, Added sugar none, Salt 1.46g.

TIP

Cook fresh fish on the day you buy it. All fresh fish should have a mild, clean smell; don't buy any with strong smelling odours. Whole fresh fish should have clear bright eyes, bright red or pink gills, shiny, undamaged bodies and close-fitting scales. White fish fillets should be a good white colour and firm-looking. They should not show any signs of dryness or discolouration, nor should they be wet and shiny.

SWEET AND SOUR PRAWNS

Simple to make, this Chinese dish is very popular in the West. It can be served as part of a Chinese meal with plain Steamed rice (page 62) or on its own as a starter for a European meal. Most Chinese recipes call for fresh, raw prawns. This is not as difficult for British cooks as in the past, when most prawns were sold cooked and often frozen as well. If you must use cooked prawns, look for the best and largest variety you can find and just heat them through instead of cooking them for the full length of time called for in the recipe. Uncooked frozen prawns are a better substitute.

Serves 4

450g/1lb fresh raw prawns, peeled and deveined (See Tip, page 12)

1½ tbsp groundnut (peanut) oil

1 tbsp finely chopped garlic

2 tsp finely chopped fresh root ginger

4 spring onions, sliced diagonally into 4cm/1½in pieces (See Tip)

1 red or green pepper (about 115g/4oz), diced into 2.5cm/1in squares

225g/8oz water chestnuts, peeled and sliced if fresh, rinsed and sliced if canned

FOR THE SAUCE

150ml/¼ pint Chicken stock (page 62)

2 tbsp Shaoxing rice wine or dry sherry

3 tbsp light soy sauce

2 tsp dark soy sauce

1½ tbsp tomato purée

3 tbsp Chinese white rice vinegar or cider vinegar

1 tbsp sugar

1 tbsp cornflour blended with 2 tbsp water

1 Pat the prawns dry with kitchen paper. Heat a wok or large frying pan until very hot, add the oil and when slightly smoking, add the garlic, ginger and spring onions and stir fry for 20 seconds. Add the prawns and stir fry for 10 seconds, then add the pepper and water chestnuts and stir fry for 30 seconds.

2 Add all the sauce ingredients to the pan, bring to the boil, reduce the heat and simmer for 4 minutes, then serve.

Nutrition notes per serving: *167 calories, Protein 12g, Carbohydrate 16g, Fat 5g, Saturated fat 1g, Fibre 1g, Added sugar 4g, Salt 1.93g.*

Ⓥ **Vegetarian option:** *substitute cubes of firm beancurd for the prawns and vegetable stock for the chicken stock.*

TIP

To diagonally slice vegetables: angle the knife or cleaver at a slant and cut evenly. The technique is used for cutting asparagus, carrots or spring onions. Its purpose is to expose more of the surface of the vegetable to the heat for quicker cooking.

QUICK PAN-FRIED FIVE-SPICE FISH

The Chinese prefer to cook fish whole although fish fillets and steaks can be satisfactorily used instead. We believe that the flesh remains moist and the flavour is best when the whole fish is used, head and tail included. To serve a fish whole is also a symbol of prosperity. The head of the fish should always point in the direction of the guest of honour, a courtesy that assures him or her of good fortune. On the way home from work, my widowed mother would often pick up a small whole fish or some fillets and quickly put together this nutritious meal. With stir-fried vegetables, yesterday's rice reheated and perhaps a Western touch of salad, you have a quick and wholesome satisfying meal. This fish also goes well with pasta. For a dinner party, try substituting fresh raw prawns for the fish fillets.

Serves 4

450g/1lb fresh fish fillets, preferably cod or haddock (See Tip, page 35)

1 tsp five-spice powder

1 tsp salt

1½ tbsp groundnut (peanut) oil

2 tbsp coarsely chopped garlic (See Tip)

2 tbsp coarsely chopped fresh root ginger

1½ tbsp Shaoxing rice wine or dry sherry

2 tsp light soy sauce

2 tsp sesame oil

rocket, to garnish

1   Rub the fish fillets with the five-spice powder and salt. Heat a wok or large frying pan until hot, then add the oil and reduce the heat. Gently pan-fry the fish on each side until lightly browned and remove from the pan with a spatula.

2   Add the garlic, ginger, rice wine, soy sauce and sesame oil to the wok, then add the fish, gently reheat and serve garnished with rocket.

Nutrition notes per serving: *157 calories, Protein 20g, Carbohydrate 2g, Fat 7g, Saturated fat 1g, Fibre 1g, Added sugar trace, Salt 1.46g.*

TIP

To peel garlic: give the garlic clove a sharp blow with the flat side of your knife or cleaver and the peel should then come off easily. Select fresh garlic which is firm and preferably pinkish in colour.

10-MINUTE SALMON WITH SPRING ONION SAUCE

We Chinese prefer that no more than a few hours elapse between the catching and cooking of fish. Indeed, in many markets in southern China and Hong Kong, fish are sold live. You can select the fish of your choice while it swims around in special glass tanks and then take it home or to a restaurant to be cooked. The accent is always on freshness. Learn to be as finicky about selecting fish and seafood as the Chinese are. It will open up a whole new world of delicious healthy eating as well as of flavour for you.Salmon's noble character lends itself to countless recipes and sauces, but I enjoy it most prepared in a simple and almost unadorned fashion, as in this recipe. The Chinese style is to consume fish neither raw nor overcooked. The aim is to capture the natural flavour, moistness and texture of the fish. The technique of steeping manages this admirably. Serve this truly quick and elegant dish as part of a main course, accompanied by an easy vegetable dish and rice, or as a starter. Sea bass or plaice fillets can be substituted.

Serves 4

450g/1lb fresh salmon fillets

2 tsp salt

½ tsp freshly ground white or black pepper

FOR THE SAUCE

6 tbsp coarsely chopped spring onions

1 tbsp finely chopped fresh root ginger (See Tip)

1½ tbsp groundnut (peanut) oil

2 tsp sesame oil

1   Rub the salmon fillets with half the salt and the pepper. Bring 600ml/1 pint of water to a simmer in a frying pan. Add the salmon, simmer for 2–3 minutes, cover tightly and turn off the heat. Leave to stand for 8 minutes.

2   Make the sauce: combine the spring onions, ginger and remaining salt in a small bowl. In a small pan, combine the oils and bring to smoking point.

3   Remove the salmon from the water and place on plate. Scatter over the spring onion mixture, then pour over the hot oils and serve.

Nutrition notes per serving: *261 calories, Protein 21g, Carbohydrate 1g, Fat 19g, Saturated fat 5g, Fibre trace, Added sugar none, Salt 2.75g.*

TIP

Fresh root ginger looks rather like a gnarled Jerusalem artichoke and ranges from 7.5–15cm/3–6in in length. It has a golden-beige, thin, dry skin that is usually peeled before use. Look for 'roots' that are firm, solid and unmarked and with no signs of shrivelling. If you store peeled fresh root ginger in a glass jar, covered in rice wine or dry sherry it will keep for several months. This has the added benefit of producing a flavoured wine that can be used in cooking.

Vegetable Dishes

COLD MARINATED BEANSPROUTS ⓥ ⓕ

This is perfect as an appetiser or as a salad course with grilled meat or fish. Although it is a bit laborious, trim the sprouts at both ends, it is well worth the effort and makes the dish look more elegant. This can be made up to four hours in advance and served cold or at room temperature.

Serves 4

450g/1lb fresh beansprouts, trimmed at both ends

2 fresh red or green chillies, seeded and finely shredded (See Tip)

3 tbsp Chinese white rice vinegar or cider vinegar

2 tbsp light soy sauce

2 tbsp finely chopped fresh coriander

2 tsp finely chopped garlic

1 Place the beansprouts and chillies in a glass bowl, then add the remaining ingredients. Mix well and leave to marinate for at least 2–3 hours, turning the beansprouts occasionally.

2 When you are ready to serve, drain the beansprouts and discard the marinade.

Nutrition notes per serving: *44 calories, Protein 4g, Carbohydrate 6g, Fat 1g, Saturated fat trace, Fibre 2g, Added sugar none, Salt 0.02g.*

TIP

To prepare fresh chillies: rinse in cold water, then, using a sharp knife, slit them lengthways. Remove and discard the seeds and rinse under cold running water before preparing according to recipe instructions. Wash your hands, knife and chopping board before preparing other foods, and be careful not to touch your eyes until you have washed your hands thoroughly with soap and water. The seeds are especially pungent and 'hot' to a fault.

STIR-FRIED BROCCOLI WITH HOISIN SAUCE ⓥ

Hoisin sauce gives a good colour and pleasant fragrance but remember a little goes a long way. Carrots or courgettes can be used, if you prefer.

Serves 4

450g/1lb fresh broccoli, broken into florets, stems peeled and sliced

1½ tbsp groundnut (peanut) oil

1 tbsp finely chopped garlic

2 tsp salt

1 tsp freshly ground black pepper

2 tbsp hoisin sauce

2 tbsp Shaoxing rice wine or dry sherry

1 Blanch the broccoli in a large pan of boiling, salted water for 5 minutes. Drain, plunge into cold water, then drain again thoroughly in a colander.

2 Heat a wok or large frying pan until it is very hot, then add the oil and when slightly smoking, add the garlic, salt, pepper and broccoli. Stir fry for 1 minute, then add the hoisin sauce, rice wine and three tablespoons of water. Continue to stir fry, over a moderately high heat for 5 minutes or until the broccoli is cooked, then serve.

Nutrition notes per serving: *98 calories, Protein 5g, Carbohydrate 5g, Fat 5g, Saturated fat 1g, Fibre 3g, Added sugar trace, Salt 2.68g.*

CRISPY 'SEAWEED' Ⓥ

This is not 'seaweed' but bok choy (Chinese white cabbage).

Serves 4

1.2kg/2½lb bok choy (Chinese white cabbage)

850ml/1½ pints groundnut (peanut) or vegetable oil

1 tsp salt

2 tsp sugar

55g/2oz lightly roasted pine nuts, to garnish

1 Preheat the oven to 250F/120C/Gas ½. Separate the stalks from the stem of the bok choy and cut the green leaves from the white stalks. Wash the leaves in several changes of cold water, drain thoroughly in a colander and dry.

2 Roll the leaves tightly and finely shred. Lay them out on a baking sheet and place in the oven for 10 minutes to dry slightly. (They should not be completely dry, or they will burn when fried.) Remove from the oven and leave to cool. (This can be done the day before.)

3 Heat a wok or deep-fat fryer until hot, add the oil and when slightly smoking, deep-fry the greens in two or three batches. When they turn deep green, this takes about 30 seconds, remove, drain well on kitchen paper and leave to cool. Toss in salt and sugar, garnish with the pine nuts and serve.

Nutrition notes per serving: *244 calories, Protein 4g, Carbohydrate 7g, Fat 22g, Saturated fat 3g, Fibre 3g, Added sugar 3g, Salt 1.28g.*

CHINESE LEAVES IN SOY SAUCE Ⓥ

This simple dish is one of my favourite ways of preparing Chinese leaves which come in various sizes – from long, compact barrel-shaped cabbages to short, squat-looking types. They are tightly packed with firm, pale green (or in some cases slightly yellow) crinkled leaves. You can also use white cabbage or any other leafy green vegetable for this dish.

Serves 2

450g/1lb Chinese leaves, cut into 4cm/1½in strips

salt

1 tbsp light soy sauce

2 tsp dark soy sauce

3 tbsp finely chopped spring onions

1 tbsp groundnut (peanut) or Chilli oil (See Tip)

1 Blanch the Chinese leaves in a pan of boiling, salted water for 5 minutes, drain thoroughly, then arrange the leaves on a warm serving plate. Drizzle over the soy sauces and spring onions.

2 Heat the oil in a wok or frying pan until it is very hot and slightly smoking, then pour over the leaves and serve.

Nutrition notes per serving: *88 calories, Protein 3g, Carbohydrate 5g, Fat 6g, Saturated fat 1g, Fibre 3g, Added sugar none, Salt 0.04g.*

TIP

For a really spicy taste, use Chilli oil instead of groundnut oil. To make Chilli oil: heat a wok or large frying pan until very hot, add 300ml/½ pint groundnut (peanut) oil and when slightly smoking, turn the heat to low. Add two tablespoons of coarsely chopped dried red chillies, including their seeds, one tablespoon of whole unroasted Sichuan peppercorns and two tablespoons of rinsed and dried whole black beans. Cook gently for 15 minutes, leave to cool undisturbed, then pour into a jar. Leave to stand for two days, then strain the oil. Stored in a tightly-sealed glass jar in a cool, dark place it will keep indefinitely.

RED-COOKED WINTER VEGETABLES Ⓥ

Red-cooking (simmering in a rich red sauce of Chinese spices) is usually reserved for meat. The technique works as well, however, with winter root vegetables, making a quick tasty stew that can be served with meat or poultry and a salad.

Serves 4

1 tbsp groundnut (peanut) oil

2 garlic cloves, crushed

2 tsp coarsely chopped fresh root ginger

450g/1lb carrots, cut into 2.5cm/1in pieces

3 tbsp hoisin sauce

1 tbsp dark soy sauce

2 tsp sugar

225g/8oz turnips, cut into 2.5cm/1in pieces

1 Heat a wok or large frying pan, then add the oil, garlic and ginger. Stir fry for 10 seconds, then add the carrots, hoisin sauce, soy sauce, sugar and 150ml/¼ pint water. Cover and cook over a high heat for 8 minutes.

2 Add the turnips and cook for 3 minutes or until the vegetables are tender. There should be very little sauce left. Transfer to a warmed dish and serve.

Nutrition notes per serving: *105 calories, Protein 2g, Carbohydrate 18g, Fat 3g, Saturated fat 1g, Fibre 4g, Added sugar 3g, Salt 0.37g.*

LETTUCE WITH OYSTER SAUCE

Lettuce prepared like this retains a crispy texture and its delicate flavour.

Serves 2–4

750g/1½lb cos or Iceberg lettuce (See Tip)

salt

3 tbsp oyster sauce

1 tbsp groundnut (peanut) oil

1 Separate the lettuce leaves, discarding any that are damaged and blanch in boiling, salted water for 30 seconds or until they have slightly wilted. Remove and drain well.

2 Mix together the oyster sauce and oil. Arrange the leaves in a warm dish, pour over the oyster sauce mixture and serve.

Nutrition notes per serving for two: *127 calories, Protein 5g, Carbohydrate 10g, Fat 8g, Saturated fat 1g, Fibre 5g, Added sugar none, Salt 2.39g.*

TIP

Separate lettuce leaves by hand. If you cut the leaves with a knife, it can discolour them. Always wash lettuce leaves in a bowl of cold water, not under running water as this can wilt them.

THREE MUSHROOM BRAISE

The three mushrooms have very different characteristics. Straw have a musky scent and meaty texture; Chinese dried are smoky-flavoured and densely textured while button are mild.

Serves 4

25g/1oz Chinese dried mushrooms (See Tip)

1 tbsp groundnut (peanut) oil

3 garlic cloves, thinly sliced

227g can Chinese straw mushrooms, drained, rinsed and left whole

85g/3oz button mushrooms, sliced

1 tbsp light soy sauce

2 tbsp Shaoxing rice wine or dry sherry

3 tbsp oyster sauce

2 tsp sugar

75ml/2½fl oz Chicken stock (page 62) or water

2 tbsp finely chopped spring onions

1 Soak the dried mushrooms in warm water for 20 minutes, then drain. Rinse well and squeeze out any excess liquid. Discard the tough stems, shred the caps and set aside.

2 Heat a wok or large frying pan until hot, add the oil and when slightly smoking, add the garlic and stir fry for 15 seconds. Add all the mushrooms and stir fry, mixing together, for a few seconds. Add the soy sauce, rice wine, oyster sauce, sugar and chicken stock. Reduce the heat and cook, stirring, for 7 minutes until the fresh mushrooms are cooked.

3 Increase the heat to high and continue to cook until most of the liquid has reduced. Mix in the spring onions and serve.

Nutrition notes per serving: *86 calories, Protein 3g, Carbohydrate 10g, Fat 3g, Saturated fat 1g, Fibre 1g, Added sugar 3g, Salt 1.27g.*

TIP

The soaking water from the Chinese dried mushrooms can be saved and used in soups or for cooking rice. Strain through a fine sieve to discard any sand or residue before using.

QUICK BEANCURD IN SPICY CHILLI SAUCE ⓥ

Any leftovers can be put into stock to make a quick soup.

Serves 4–6

1 tbsp groundnut (peanut) oil

1 tbsp coarsely chopped garlic

2 tsp finely chopped fresh root ginger

3 tbsp chopped spring onions

1 tbsp whole yellow bean sauce

1 tbsp tomato purée

2 tsp chilli bean sauce

2 tsp dark soy sauce

2 tsp sugar

2 tsp sesame oil

450g/1lb firm beancurd, cut into 1cm/½in dice (See Tip, page 16)

1 Heat a wok or large frying pan, then add the oil, garlic, ginger and spring onions and stir fry for 30 seconds. Add all the reamaining ingredients, except the beancurd, and simmer for 5 minutes.

2 Add the beancurd to the sauce, simmer for 3 minutes, then serve.

Nutrition notes per serving for four: *142 calories, Protein 9g, Carbohydrate 6g, Fat 9g, Saturated fat 1g, Fibre 1g, Added sugar 3g, Salt 0.11g.*

Rice & Noodles

CURRIED FRIED RICE WITH GREEN BEANS ⓥ

In this dish, the cooked rice can be stir-fried immediately, without waiting for it to cool.

Serves 4

2 tbsp groundnut (peanut) oil

115g/4oz Chinese long beans, runner or French beans, trimmed and diced

1 quantity cooked long grain rice (page 62)

1 tbsp finely chopped garlic

3 tbsp chopped fresh coriander

grated rind ½ lime

2 dried chillies, seeded and chopped

2 tbsp light soy sauce

2 tsp sugar

2 tbsp curry paste

½ tsp salt

1 Heat a wok or large frying pan, add the oil and when moderately hot, add the beans and stir fry for 2 minutes. Add the rice and stir fry for 3 minutes. Stir in the remaining ingredients and mix thoroughly. Cook, stirring continuously, for a further 5 minutes, then serve.

Nutrition notes per serving: *409 calories, Protein 7g, Carbohydrate 81g, Fat 8g, Saturated fat 1g, Fibre 2g, Added sugar 3g, Salt 0.93g.*

TIP

'Easy-cook' and pre-cooked long grain rice are unsuitable for recipes in this book. Try to find Thai aromatic long grain rice which has a pleasing fragrance.

TWO MUSHROOM RICE ⓥ ⓕ

This is a simple vegetarian adaptation of a traditional chicken-rice-mushroom dish.

Serves 4

25g/1oz Chinese dried mushrooms

1 tbsp groundnut (peanut) oil

3 tbsp finely chopped spring onions

½ tsp salt

225g/8oz button mushrooms, quartered

long grain rice measured to the 450ml/16fl oz mark in a measuring jug (See Tip)

2 tbsp light soy sauce

1 Soak the dried mushrooms in 850ml/1½ pints of very hot water for 20 minutes until soft. Remove with a slotted spoon and reserve the soaking liquid. Squeeze out any excess liquid, discard the stalks and cut the caps into quarters.
2 Heat a wok or large frying pan, add the oil and when slightly smoking, add the spring onions, salt and button mushrooms and stir fry for 2 minutes. Add the dried mushrooms and stir fry for 1 minute or until all the liquid has evaporated. Remove and set aside.
3 Place the rice in a pan, add the mushrooms, soy sauce and reserved soaking liquid and bring to the boil. Continue boiling until most of the surface liquid has evaporated (15–20 minutes). Cover the pan with a very tight-fitting lid, turn the heat as low as possible and cook the rice, undisturbed, for 15–20 minutes.

Nutrition notes per serving: *372 calories, Protein 8g, Carbohydrate 81g, Fat 4g, Saturated fat 1g, Fibre 1g, Added sugar none, Salt 0.65g.*

FRIED RICE ✸

In China, fried rice is eaten as a 'filler' at the end of a dinner party. It is not eaten with other dishes in place of steamed rice, although many Westerners do enjoy it because it does go with almost any Chinese dish. Long grain rice is the most popular for cooking in southern China and it is my favourite, too. It needs to be washed before it is cooked. Do not confuse it with the 'easy-cook' and pre-cooked varieties which are now widely available as these are unsuitable for Chinese cooking. They lack the starchy flavour, texture and clean white colour which is so essential to Chinese cuisine.

Serves 4

115g/4oz fresh peas or frozen peas, thawed

2 eggs, beaten

2 tsp sesame oil

2 tbsp groundnut (peanut) oil

long grain rice measured to the 400ml/14fl oz mark on a measuring jug, cooked according to method on page 62 and left to go cold

55g/2oz cooked ham, finely diced

2 tsp salt

½ tsp freshly ground black pepper

3 tbsp finely chopped spring onions, white part only

115g/4oz fresh beansprouts

2 tbsp finely chopped spring onions, to garnish

1 If using fresh peas, blanch in a pan of boiling water for 5 minutes, then drain. Mix together the eggs and sesame oil and set aside.

2 Heat a wok or large frying pan until very hot, add the oil and when slightly smoking, add the cooked, cooled rice and stir fry for 3 minutes. Add the ham, peas, salt and pepper and stir fry for 5 minutes over a high heat.

3 Add the egg mixture and stir fry for 1 minute, then add the spring onions and beansprouts and stir fry for 2 minutes or until the eggs have set. Transfer to a warm plate, garnish with the spring onions and serve hot or cool as a rice salad.

Nutrition notes per serving: *429 calories, Protein 14g, Carbohydrate 72g, Fat 11g, Saturated fat 2g, Fibre 2g, Added sugar none, Salt 3.01g.*

✸ *Cool quickly, then freeze. Can be frozen for up to 1 month. To serve, defrost in the fridge.*

TIP

Fried rice is common in Chinese restaurants, but it is frequently incorrectly cooked. If you follow these simple guidelines, you will be rewarded with perfect fried rice as it should be. The cooked long grain rice should be thoroughly cool, preferably cold, before you start preparing Fried rice. Once cooled, much of the moisture in the rice evaporates, allowing the oil to coat the dry grains and prevent them from sticking. Store the cooked rice in the fridge until you are ready to use it. Never put any soy sauce into Fried rice. This not only colours the rice unnaturally but makes it too salty. Any moisture will also make the rice gummy. Fried rice should always be quite dry and the grains quite separate. Always be sure the oil is hot enough to avoid saturating the boiled or steamed plain rice. Saturated rice is greasy and heavy. The finished rice should have a wonderful smoky taste and flavour.

CHOW MEIN

Chinese noodles are incredibly varied. They come in all shapes and sizes and are most commonly made from wheat or rice flour and water and, in the south, from wheat flour, water and eggs. Hand-made noodles are formed by an elaborate but rapid process of kneading, pulling, tossing and twisting the dough into a cascade of fine long noodles. This spectacular skill takes four to five years to acquire and is a delight to watch. Noodles play an important part in Chinese tradition since they are a symbol of longevity and it is considered bad luck to cut them since this might shorten one's life! Chow mein literally means 'stir-fried noodles'. Almost any ingredient, such as fish, meat, poultry or vegetables, can be added. In China, it is a popular lunch dish, either served at the end of the meal or eaten by itself. It also makes a tasty noodle salad if served cold.

Serves 4

225g/8oz dried or fresh egg noodles (See Tip)

1 tbsp sesame oil, plus 3 tsp

115g skinless chicken breasts, sliced into fine 5cm/2in long shreds

4 tsp light soy sauce

2 tsp Shaoxing rice wine or dry sherry, plus 1 tbsp

1½ tsp salt

1 tsp freshly ground white pepper

2½ tbsp groundnut (peanut) oil

1 tbsp finely chopped garlic

55g/2oz mangetout, trimmed

55g/2oz Parma ham or cooked ham, finely shredded

2 tsp dark soy sauce

½ tsp sugar

3 tbsp finely chopped spring onions

1   Cook dried noodles according to packet instructions, or in boiling water for 4–5 minutes, and fresh noodles for 3–5 minutes. Drain, then plunge into cold water. Drain thoroughly and toss in one tablespoon of sesame oil.

2   Combine the chicken shreds with half the light soy sauce, two teaspoons of rice wine, one teaspoon of sesame oil, half a teaspoon of salt and half the pepper. Mix well and marinate for 20 minutes.

3   Heat a wok or large frying pan until very hot, add one tablespoon of groundnut oil and when slightly smoking, add the chicken and stir fry the mixture for 2 minutes. Transfer to a plate and wipe the wok or pan clean.

4   Reheat the wok or pan until very hot, add the remaining groundnut oil and when slightly smoking, add the garlic and stir fry for 10 seconds. Add the mangetout and ham and stir fry for 1 minute. Add the noodles, remaining light soy sauce, the dark soy sauce, remaining rice wine, salt and pepper, the sugar and spring onions and continue to stir fry for 2 minutes.

5   Return the chicken and any juices to the pan and stir fry for 3–4 minutes or until the chicken is cooked. Stir in the remaining sesame oil, give a few final stirs, then serve.

Nutrition notes per serving: *393 calories, Protein 19g, Carbohydrate 43g, Fat 16g, Saturated fat 3g, Fibre 1g, Added sugar 1g, Salt 2.83g.*

TIP

Rounded noodles are best for stir frying or pan-frying, while flat egg noodles are usually used in soups. Fresh noodles are suitable for freezing. Simply defrost thoroughly before cooking. If you want to cook noodles in advance, cover with plastic wrap at the end of Step 1 and place in the fridge. They remain usable for

SINGAPORE NOODLES

Curry is not original to Chinese cuisine. It was introduced to China centuries ago by immigrants returning home from sojourns in South-east Asia, especially from the east coast of India. Serve these noodles with a fish or meat dish or just by themselves. This dish is also wonderful cold.

Serves 4–6

225g/8oz dried thin rice noodles

55g/2oz dried Chinese black mushrooms

4 eggs, beaten

1 tbsp sesame oil

1 tsp salt

½ tsp freshly ground white pepper

3 tbsp groundnut (peanut) oil

1½ tbsp finely chopped garlic

1 tbsp chopped fresh root ginger

6 fresh red or green chillies, seeded and finely shredded (See Tip, page 43)

6 water chestnuts, peeled if fresh, rinsed if canned

115g/4oz Chinese barbecue pork or cooked ham, finely shredded

3 spring onions, finely shredded

115g/4oz small peeled cooked prawns

175g/6oz frozen small garden peas or petits pois, thawed

fresh coriander, to garnish

FOR THE CURRY SAUCE

2 tbsp light soy sauce

3 tbsp Indian madras curry paste or 2 tbsp powder

2 tbsp Shaoxing rice wine or dry sherry

1 tbsp sugar

1 tsp salt

1 tsp freshly ground black pepper

250ml can coconut milk (See Tip)

175ml/6fl oz Chicken stock (page 62)

1 Soak the rice noodles in a bowl of warm water for 25 minutes, then drain in a colander or sieve.

2 Soak the mushrooms in water for 20 minutes, drain and squeeze out excess liquid. Remove and discard the stems and finely shred the caps into thin strips.

3 Combine the eggs with the sesame oil, salt and pepper and set aside.

4 Heat a wok or large frying pan until very hot, add the oil and when slightly smoking, add the garlic, ginger and chillies and stir fry for 30 seconds. Add the water chestnuts, mushrooms, pork or ham and spring onions and stir fry for 1 minute. Add the rice noodles, prawns and peas and stir fry for 2 minutes.

5 Add all the sauce ingredients to the pan and cook over a high heat for 5 minutes or until most of the liquid has evaporated. Pour in the egg mixture, stir frying constantly, until the eggs set. Transfer to a warm platter, garnish and serve.

Nutrition notes per serving for four: *627 calories, Protein 32g, Carbohydrate 68g, Fat 26g, Saturated fat 5g, Fibre 7g, Added sugar 4g, Salt 4.64g.*

Ⓥ **Vegetarian option:** *eliminate the meat and prawns and use more coconut milk in place of the chicken stock.*

TIP

Shake cans of coconut milk well before opening. Any leftover can be kept in the fridge for a week out of its can. You can make your own coconut milk by soaking fresh grated flesh or desiccated coconut in boiling water to cover for 30 minutes. Leave until cool, then squeeze through muslin. Blocks of coconut cream can be dissolved in a little boiling water and powdered coconut milk is also available.

HOT BEAN THREAD NOODLES

Bean thread, or cellophane noodles are delightfully light. They are very fine, white and almost transparent. Unlike other types of noodles, they can be successfully reheated.

Serves 4

115g/4oz bean thread noodles

1 tbsp groundnut (peanut) oil

3 tbsp finely chopped spring onions

2 tbsp finely chopped garlic

450g minced beef

2 tsp coarsely chopped spring onions, to garnish

FOR THE SAUCE

450ml/16fl oz Chicken stock (page 62)

1½ tbsp chilli bean sauce

1 tbsp whole yellow bean sauce

2 tbsp light soy sauce

2 tbsp dark soy sauce

½ tsp salt

½ tsp freshly ground black pepper

2 tsp sesame oil

1 Soak the noodles in a large bowl of warm water for 15 minutes. When soft, drain and discard the water. Cut into 7.5cm/3in lengths using scissors or a knife.

2 Heat a wok or large frying pan until very hot, add the oil and when slightly smoking, add the spring onions and garlic and stir fry for 15 seconds. Add the meat and stir fry for 8 minutes or until cooked.

3 Add all the sauce ingredients, except the sesame oil, to the pan and cook over a gentle heat for 5 minutes. Add the noodles and sesame oil and cook for a further 5 minutes or until most of the liquid has evaporated. Ladle into individual bowls, garnish and serve.

Nutrition notes per serving: *319 calories, Protein 28g, Carbohydrate 27g, Fat 12g, Saturated fat 3g, Fibre 1g, Added sugar none, Salt 1.26g.*

TIP

A good technique for separating bean thread noodle strands when weighing them out is to pull them apart in a large paper or plastic bag. This stops them from flying all over the place.

SPINACH AND RICE NOODLES ⓥ

Unlike egg noodles, rice noodles do not become sticky and gummy when they are moist, making them convenient to serve cold.

Serves 2–4

115g/4oz rice noodles

1 tbsp groundnut (peanut) oil

1 tsp salt

2 tbsp coarsely chopped garlic

700g/1lb 9oz fresh spinach, stalks removed

2 tsp sugar

1 tbsp light soy sauce

2 tsp Chilli oil (See Tip, page 44)

1 Soak the rice noodles in a bowl of warm water for 25 minutes, then drain in a colander or sieve.

2 Heat a wok or large frying pan to a moderate heat, add the oil and stir fry the salt and garlic for a few seconds. Add the spinach leaves and stir fry for 2 minutes to coat thoroughly. When the spinach has wilted to about a third of its original size, add the noodles, sugar, soy sauce and chilli oil and continue to stir   fry   for 4 minutes. Pour off any excess liquid and serve hot or cold.

Nutrition notes per serving for two: *426 calories, Protein 18g, Carbohydrate 58g, Fat 15g, Saturated fat 2g, Fibre 10g, Added sugar 5g, Salt 3.72g.*

Desserts

LYCHEES WITH PAPAYA SAUCE ⓕ

Lychees are a sweet exotic fruit becoming more available in the West. Try to use fresh ones in this elegant dessert.

Serves 4–6

1 x 450g/1lb papaya

2 tbsp sugar

450g/1lb fresh lychees, peeled and stone or canned lychees, drained

1 Slice the papaya in half lengthways and remove the seeds. Peel away the skin and cut the flesh into slices. Purée the slices in a food processor or blender, then stir in the sugar. Spoon a little papaya sauce on to a plate and top with lychees.

Nutrition notes per serving for four: *111 calories, Protein 1g, Carbohydrate 28g, Fat 1g, Saturated fat none, Fibre 3g, Added sugar 8g, Salt 0.02g.*

TIP

When buying papaya look for fruit that is ripe. The skin will be yellow and the fruit will feel slighty soft. Choose lychees with the pinkest skins, avoid any with shrivelled, dry skins.

MANGO FOOL

This rich and refreshing dessert brings a meal to a close with a South-east Asian touch.

Serves 4

450g/1lb fresh mangoes, peeled and sliced (See Tip, page 32)

2 tbsp sugar

250ml/9fl oz double or whipping cream

1 Purée the mangoes in a food processor or blender, then push through a fine sieve and stir in the sugar.

2 Whip the cream until it forms stiff peaks, then gently fold into the mango purée. This will keep for 3–4 hours, covered with plastic wrap, in the fridge.

Nutrition notes per serving: *374 calories, Protein 2g, Carbohydrate 25g, Fat 30g, Saturated fat 19g, Fibre 3g, Added sugar 8g, Salt 0.06g.*

Basic Recipes

QUICK AND EASY CHICKEN STOCK

Makes 1.2 litres/2 pints

900g chicken wings

3 slices fresh root ginger, cut into 5x1cm/2x½in diagonal slices

4 spring onions, cut into thirds and green tops discarded

2 large garlic cloves, skins on and crushed

2 tsp salt

1 Place the chicken wings in a large pan, cover with 1.4 litres/2½ pints of water and bring to simmering point.
2 As the water begins to simmer, gently skim off the scum that rises to the surface, using a large flat spoon. Add the remaining ingredients and partially cover. Gently simmer for 1 hour.
3 Strain the stock through a fine-meshed sieve, leave to cool, then chill and remove any surface fat. It is now ready for use.

❄ *Cool thoroughly before transferring to containers and freezing. Defrost thoroughly in the fridge.*

STEAMED RICE

Serves 4

long grain rice to fill a measuring jug to the 400m/14fl oz level

1 Place the rice in a large bowl and wash it in several changes of water until the water runs clear. Drain and place in a heavy pan with 600ml/1 pint of water and bring to the boil.
2 Continue boiling until most of the surface liquid has evaporated. This takes about 15 minutes. (The surface of the rice should have small indentations like a pitted crater.) At this point, cover with a very tight-fitting lid, reduce the heat as low as possible and let it cook, undisturbed, for 15 minutes.
3 Remove the pan from the heat and let it rest for 5 minutes before serving. There is no need to 'fluff' the rice.

SWEET AND SOUR SAUCE

Ideal for any deep-fried foods, this keeps well in a tightly-sealed jar in the fridge.

2 tbsp ginger marmalade

2 tbsp orange marmalade

1 tsp salt

3 tbsp Chinese white rice vinegar or cider vinegar

2 tbsp tomato ketchup

1 Combine all the ingredients together and mix thoroughly. Transfer to a small dish to serve or place in a jar and chill until needed.